A TRUE STORY

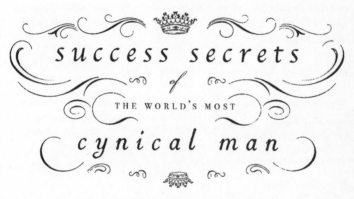

success secrets

of

THE WORLD'S MOST

cynical man

K. SOLOMON

Published by
THOMAS NELSON
Since 1798

www.thomasnelson.com

Written by Max Davis

Cover Design: The Designworks Group | Jason Gabbert | www.thedesignworksgroup.com
Interior Design: Kimberly Sagmiller, VisibilityCreative.com

ISBN 10: 1-59145-564-2
ISBN 13: 978-1-59145-564-6

Printed and bound in the United States of America

table of contents

- prologue -

In a world like ours, someone has to be blunt. So do not be offended by my bluntness, because bluntness is one of my gifts. I wish someone had been blunt with me. It would have saved me a lot of time, and time is a commodity never to be wasted. You see, time is *the* most precious commodity—even more so than money—because you can always make more money, but you can't make more time. There're only so many seconds in a day, and they're ticking away at light speed, never to be retrieved or invested again.

So instead of taking forever to get around to what I mean, I choose to just be blunt. I just give the *bottom-line*—results. When I set out to get a job done, I never wasted time announcing to the world what I was *going* to do; I rolled up my sleeves and got to work. That's one reason I accomplished so much in my lifetime.

I guess it would be fair to call me a mover and a shaker. When I move, things shake, and results happen. And I saw a lot of results in my life. In fact, because of my extraordinary work ethic and insight, I became the richest man to have ever lived.

To give you an idea of the staggering amount of wealth I accumulated, Bill Gates, Warren Buffet, Sam Walton, Donald Trump, and even King Tut himself are mere novices compared to me. Now, I'll be the first to admit that I had the advantage of being born with the proverbial silver spoon in my mouth (although it was actually gold), but don't let anyone try and tell you otherwise—it was through my own insight, strategic planning, and unyielding work ethic that my empire grew into one of the most powerful and magnificent on record.

In addition to making an astonishing amount of wealth, my resume included a long list of other impressive achievements. As my nation's leader, I established long-lasting security and built its most profitable trade alliances ever. I was also a diplomat, creating a host of innovative treaties between some of the world's most warlike countries.

My architectural genius went unmatched. Wright and Palladio have nothing on me. I was responsible for designing and overseeing the construction of palaces, temples, estates, botanical gardens, bridges, whole infrastructures, and government buildings that rival the Notre Dame Cathedral or Taj Mahal.

When it comes to *worldly* success, I'll put my portfolio up against anyone in the world—past or present.

So you would do well to listen to my advice, because I know what I'm talking about. Don't be one of those puffed-up know-it-alls who actually believe they have it all together. Only a fool does that. A clever man, on the other hand, regards highly the advice from wise counselors. Besides, why would anyone *not* listen to someone who has already succeeded and accomplished what I have?

Do yourself a favor. Save some heartache and money and don't reinvent the wheel.

Listen to me.

What I'm going to tell you didn't come from some four-eyed professor in a class at one of those idealistic universities with ivy-covered walls. I didn't learn any of this from self-help books or on pop-psychology talk shows. I earned this practical, no-nonsense, where-the-rubber-meets-the-road knowledge the hard way.

There I am being blunt again. I was more politically correct in my younger days—but not necessarily wiser.

Before you read any further, however, there are a couple things I must warn you about. If you are the type that gets his feathers ruffled easily, you might want to get another book—one that's just going to tell you what you want to hear—because I can make no such promise. On the other hand, if you're someone that values the *bottom-line*, as I did, then I think you'll be glad you kept reading because you probably need to hear what I have to say. No, I take that back—I *know* you need to hear what I have to say.

World leaders and prominent figures traveled from all over the globe to hear what I have to say. They gave me a plethora of exotic and priceless gifts in exchange for my counsel. I would never have charged them, but they would gladly pay if I requested it.

Some even said I was the wisest man that has ever lived. The way I see it, if world leaders and prominent figures took their time and spent fortunes to hear my words of wisdom, the few bucks you shelled out and the short time you're investing in this book is a great deal, because I'm going to give you what I gave them—the *bottom-line*.

I realize that it may be difficult for you to conceive of the amount of wealth and knowledge I possessed. You're probably tempted to suppose it's all a fabrication or at best an exaggeration. But it is neither. As unbelievable as it may seem, it is actually true. I possessed all the things that man yearns for—power, wealth, fame, freedom, influence, and knowledge. My life was an amazing fantasy, infinitely above and beyond what most could only imagine. And because of all this success, it might be somewhat of a surprise when I tell you that in addition to being exceedingly wise and wealthy, I am also *dreadfully cynical*. You could call me "cynically wise."

Cynicism has not always been my way, however. Its seed was conceived in me upon the fateful realization that success that I've been telling you about is a fantasy—it is absolutely *worthless*. I know. I know. I'm getting ahead of myself–and not being as blunt as I promised, but I'm putting it on the table now.

Despite reaching these monumental goals and seeing the fulfillment of lifelong dreams that I was thoroughly convinced would bring lasting satisfaction, I found just the opposite to be true. Instead of satisfaction, I found I was left with a cold, futile emptiness. But this is nothing new. History is littered with the disillusionment of the successful.

For example, President Thomas Jefferson commissioned a man named Meriwether Lewis to lead an amazing expedition to explore the immense wilderness that stretched from the Mississippi River to the Pacific Ocean–something no one had done before. A man's man, and one who longed for adventure, Lewis was obsessed with being successful in his mission.

After he reached his goal, however, at the pinnacle of his success, he wrote: "I feel all that restlessness...which

I cannot help but thinking proceeds from that void in our hearts. Whence it comes I know not, but certain it is, that I never felt less like a hero than at the present moment." Not long afterward, Lewis committed suicide.

Like Lewis, as the fantasy of my life began to wither before my eyes, I fell helplessly into the dark pit of depression—a fall that vast riches and lofty accomplishments did little to slow. Once I even found myself—the man with literally everything—staring out the window of one of my fabulous towers, surveying the beauty of the kingdom I had toiled to build, seriously contemplating jumping.

Though the thoughts of suicide tormented my mind, deep down I guess I knew that I'd never actually go through with the act. My strict religious tradition frowns heavily on such an act of ultimate self-destruction. However, I identified with Thoreau: "Most men lead lives of quiet desperation." Yes, I was in desperate straits. Like everything else in my life, my mid-life crisis was also extreme.

At that point in my existence, everything seemed utterly meaningless to me. All that I'd accomplished, every single bit of it, I saw as vanity. Nothing mattered–absolutely nothing–and the satisfaction I so desperately yearned for somehow eluded me. For all my labor and sweat under the sun, what did I *really* have? How much of it could I take with me to the grave? We slave our whole lives to make something of ourselves, and, in the end, what do we get from the struggle?

We end up six feet under in a box covered with dirt.

I felt as if my life were a mere speck in the limitless sea of time–here for a moment and then gone like dust in the wind. I was no different than the other billions of human beings coming and going, merely existing, scratching and clawing, and doing whatever they can to survive on this earth. And for what? Everyone fades into nothingness and is eventually forgotten.

Life seemed like one, big, pointless cycle—the sun rising and setting, completing its same course over and over again, the wind traveling from north to south and back again. Rivers flowing into the sea, giving its water; the sea then sends the water up into the clouds, which rain down back into the rivers.

Nature, like the rest of us, goes through its mundane motions of life, its endless cycles.

Our meager number of days, I thought, may be occupied with busy-ness and the chasing of well-conceived goals, but it is all for naught. Like a revolving door in time, we are born and die, and future generations will remember our achievements vaguely—if at all.

In my despair, I longed for the *bottom-line* of life. I craved truth. But what was "truth"? Does such a thing even exist?

In all my wisdom, I wrestled with life's questions: What was life's ultimate meaning? Why are we on this planet, anyway? Is it possible to find genuine purpose and fulfillment, or is life just the cruel result of some cosmic accident?

Desperate for answers, I did something really radical that few people ever have the opportunity to do: I changed my entire life course and set out on an extensive quest to find the upshot of life. After all, I had the resources to make such a quest possible. Equipped with the tools of freedom, power, wealth, and influence, nothing was out of my reach. So, with unyielding resolve and a heightened work ethic, I put my plan in action to learn and experience all I could conceive that life had to offer.

I determined that nothing short of answers would satisfy me, and I was steadfast in my commitment—I wanted results. Along each leg of the journey, I carefully weighed the value of all my experiences in the balance of my understanding.

The volume you are holding in your hands is the

result of that search for answers. In it are some rare nuggets of wisdom that surprised even me. I urge you to pay attention to them, to listen closely to my words. If you do, my words will affect your life as profoundly as they did mine—and that is a guarantee.

LESSON I

Cynicism will come to everyone who searches
for truth—and can be a helpful friend.

CHAPTER I

getting it wrong

Where did I go wrong? I asked myself while contemplating my state of melancholy. Can you imagine me–as successful as I was–even asking such a question?

Where did I go wrong?

It was a preposterous question, because I built my whole life on making the right choices and on helping other people do the same. That's what it's all about, right–making good choices? That's what we drill into our kids' heads from the time they can crawl until we give them the boot out of the house–"If you make good choices in life, little Johnny, then life will go well and you will be happy."

Well, to that I say, "Utter rubbish!" It's a bunch of lies. I made good choices, and they left me cynical and keenly aware of how meaningless life can be. Where was all that happiness? If success equaled happiness, then I should have been the happiest man in history, because I sure was the richest and most successful! Yet, despite having it all, I could find nothing about my dreary existence to be happy about.

And what exactly is happiness, anyway?

Do we even *have* a choice in the matter, as some say, or are we merely pawns, preordained to live out a fate already mapped out for us? Is there really such a thing as *free will*?

I kept asking myself if I was truly the one responsible for the glut of achievements that I've been boasting about or if it was all just pure luck. My outward success may have suggested it, yet my inner turmoil was something beyond my ability to control. No matter how hard I tried to suppress it—like waves that endlessly batter the seashore—hopelessness kept coming back again and again, slowly eroding the fabric of my being.

If my success was only luck, sometimes I think my luck was actually a curse.

Now, I can just hear you saying, "Why are you complaining? I'd trade my paltry life with yours any day. I would love to see what it's like to experience such problems!"

My response to that is: Don't be too quick to utter your shallow desires before God. You may get your wish one day and be sorry.

Take the lottery for example—a concept I find quite disturbing. Seventy percent of lottery winners are bankrupt within a few short years, and most look back to curse the day they won. One man called his winnings of sixteen million dollars the "Lottery of Death." Another, who had won over $300 million, said, "I should have ripped up the ticket and burned it!" Just think if they had won serious amounts of money.

These don't sound like happy people. Oh, but your situation would be different, I'm sure. Me, I can absolutely relate, because I know first-hand that everything we are told about being rich is a *lie*.

I had everything–all the stuff anyone could ever want. Yet contentment eluded me. I counseled others about their problems and gave sage advice, but I could not make myself happy or content.

Instead, I found my restlessness ever increasing. And for all the knowledge that I supposedly possessed, the knowledge I desperately needed in order to calm my soul completely escaped me.

This was precisely why the first item on my quest's agenda was to acquire more of what I felt I was lacking– knowledge.

Yes, more knowledge was the answer. It had worked for me in the past. In my earlier years, when I had asked God for wisdom, He granted it, and I became wise beyond my seventeen years with the aptitude to lead an entire nation. Over the years, I built the foundation of my success on that wisdom.

Now, I reasoned, if I could only expand my intellect, then more understanding would come and I would at last have satisfaction. With that, I decided to apply my mind with great diligence to the arduous task of studying and learning all that I possibly could of the intellects of man—philosophy, science, world religions, and so forth.

At first, I must admit, the experience of learning new theories and concepts did give me a heightened sense of stimulation. It seemed to endow me with a cultured clout that placed me above the ignorant, gullible masses.

But this too was an illusion. Eventually, the novelty wore off, and my stimulation turned to agitation as the studying became a grueling and grievous undertaking. Too much study simply wears out the mind, especially when the effort leads you to where it led me—to the understanding that there is really nothing new out there.

Most of man's learning is the same old information rehashed, repackaged, and recycled. New books come out year after year—stacks upon stacks, rows upon rows—but there's virtually nothing *new* in any of them! Currently, there are over 120,000 books published each year. It's ludicrous.

It shook me to my core, however, when I discovered that the more intellectual a man is the more depressing things really get! More knowledge opens you up to see how mixed up this world actually is. There are injustices going on all around, from the tiniest insects killing and devouring each other to the rich and powerful running over the poor and taking advantage of them. What an incredible imbalance of wealth and power there is in the world! Masses are starving and doing without things they urgently need while fat cats like me have more than they could ever possibly need. Where's the justice in that?

I tell you, this whole world system is screwed up. It is twisted, but you can't straighten it out regardless of how hard you try. Having more knowledge about the situation is not going to help either. I know this may be a hard blow to politicians, business tycoons, and even many clergy because it means all their attempts to change the world mean *absolutely nothing*! But most of you won't accept that and will try anyway.

My cynicism grew when I saw injustices that went unanswered and that people routinely deny truth. Increasing my intellect only increased my cynicism and did nothing to help solve any of my emotional problems. The more knowledge I attained, the more the simpleton living his base existence appealed to me.

Ignorance really is bliss. Have you ever noticed that the mentally disabled are usually very happy people?

They don't even realize they are impaired and walk around with big smiles plastered across their faces. Ah, to be free from the heaviness that comes with too much knowledge!

People are addicted to amusement because it suspends their minds—that's what the word "amusement" means; no thinking. People don't want to think about how painful their lives really are. They just want to forget their problems, even if it may be for only a few idyllic moments at a time. Knowing too much only keeps the pain in front of you.

For centuries education has touted itself as the universal solution for everything from criminal behavior to societal harmony, but it's the biggest farce of all time. Even after the Age of Enlightenment, the Industrial Revolution, and the age of technology, the world is just as depraved as it has ever been—maybe even worse. Murder and rape still abound. Child molesters roam the streets. Corrupt leaders are responsible for the slaughter and starvation of millions. Shady politicians and businessmen dominate the headlines.

The fact is, man has always been sinful and always will be. That's just the way things are. With more technology and medication, there are simply more things to get addicted to. I'm not denying that education has helped keep us healthy, comfortable, and informed, but it has done nothing to fix the universal hole in man's soul.

More education may improve the quality of life, but it will never bestow significance or purpose. Nor can it solve the evils of the world.

On the heels of the anguish brought on by my increased knowledge came madness and folly. Those who pursue knowledge for the sake of knowledge will eventually go this way. One sure-fire way of discerning that a person is not an intellectual is when he *thinks* he is. Because intellectualism eventually puffs a person up with arrogance, it most often leads him to ridiculous conclusions. George Orwell said, "Some ideas are so absurd that only an intellectual could believe them."

The world is full of educated fools, and I was becoming one of them.

At the end of your life, whether you are highly educated with a string of degrees behind your name or illiterate will make absolutely no difference, because when they toss that dirt on top of your grave, your knowledge or the lack of it will not help. Nor will they ever give meaning to life.

Ludwig Wittgenstein, a fellow genius and author and utterly depressed man, said, "*Why is philosophy so complicated? It ought to be entirely simple. Philosophy unties the knots in our thinking that we have, in a senseless way, put there. To do this it must make movements that are just as complicated as these knots."* Did he sound confused? He must have been, because after all his searching he finally committed suicide. I guess he never found the answer—or maybe he did.

He and I could have been pals, because like him, every time I thought I had found the bottom-line answer through intellectualism, it somehow proved elusive. It was like trying to catch the wind. Have you ever tried to do that? Go outside and try to grab a handful of wind. It's impossible. You can't do it. Attempting to find the bottom-line through the intellect will only frustrate you.

However, there is one thing intellectualism can do for you. It will help you enunciate your misery with more eloquence.

LESSON 2

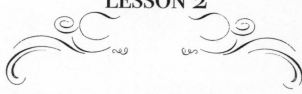

Intelligence is overrated. Knowledge can be used for good or bad. The world needs wisdom.

CHAPTER 2

are we hearing truth yet ?

Bone weary from studying and now even more depressed, I put the books aside and sought to refresh myself with good times—to try some amusement for myself. I didn't want to over-think my existence anymore; I just wanted to *feel good.* Filling my life with pleasure would force the depression right out. It would have to. After all, you can't feel good and be in pain at the same time, right? I'd kick back and enjoy the journey to the fullest. Since we are going to die anyway and you can't take anything with you, why not fill your days with as much gusto as possible? After all, you only go around once.

The promises held out by hedonism were so enticing that I jumped in with both feet. I wanted to fly free and taste it all—no rules and no restrictions; only liberty. I refused my heart no pleasure and denied myself nothing my eyes desired. I tasted of a plethora of delights—some we will discuss later in the chapter—but there was one particular pleasure that differed from all the rest: sexual pleasure. And because of those differences, I want to take a deeper look at this matter first.

Sexual pleasure is unlike any other pleasure because it manipulates man's natural cravings, dangling the carrot of the ultimate physical euphoria. These fantasies lock on to our biological urges and give birth to an unmanageable beast. Pornographers have known this for centuries and have exploited it.

Society creates characters like James Bond, with his dashing looks, exciting life on the edge, and unconstrained love life with exotic women. Entertainers have created characters such as this because we somehow believe their lifestyles are the ultimate–especially the part about the women. We somehow think that we would be truly happy if we could experience one beautiful woman after another with no responsibility or guilt.

Ah, to experience the perfect woman...or *many* perfect women!

There is one problem–*she doesn't exist.* This too is an illusion. Like a mirage in the desert, such entertainers present a promise no real woman can give. And those who present themselves as perfect, the ultimate goal, are lying–she promises to quench your thirst, but instead she will leave you with nothing but sand in your mouth.

If anyone should know this, it's me. I've dipped in the well of love with hundreds of women–so many that after a while I could hardly tell them apart.

A recent autobiography comes to mind about a certain well-known professional athlete. In that book, he describes his frequent sexual relations with women. He bragged that he basically had them at his beck-and-call twenty-four hours a day, seven days a week. Well, just as I previously stated regarding my portfolio, my exploits with women are no different. Not a single professional athlete, rock star, actor, or even James Bond himself—if he were real—can come close to my sexual exploits.

Literally, all I had to do is snap my fingers and women were delivered to me. And I snapped my fingers a *lot*—hundreds and hundreds of times. It's no secret that I loved women; I had quite a reputation as a womanizer. I've held them in my arms, taken in their fragrance, tasted their lips, and shared the act of sexual intercourse with the most glamorous and exotic women of the world—from the cute girl next door to the mystical foreigner.

I had a smorgasbord of personalities, curves, skin tones, hair, and eye colors available to me. Whatever my fantasy, whatever my mood, I could satisfy any sexual impulse on a whim. Self-control or delayed gratification did not enter my mind.

I can almost see some of you men out there drooling, thinking, "What a lucky guy. You're killing me with all your *problems*!" But hear me on this, and hear me well— if my experience taught me one thing, it's that charm is deceitful and beauty is fleeting. Being in the arms of a gorgeous woman is not all it's cracked up to be. It's actually overrated. The idea that somehow sex with many different women—or simply with a woman different from the one you have—is ultimately satisfying is a joke.

Like everything else, even sex eventually gets old. And as enticing as it is and as good as it feels licentious sex never satisfies. Lust is never satisfied. It's a raging fire that goes forever unquenched. Instead of satisfying, each episode only exacerbates the hunger and makes desires worse.

When a person lives for this type of pleasure, you eventually reach a point where bondage overtakes enjoyment. There's an allurement about illicit sex that keeps a person strung along, always craving more. It's addictive, but it eventually becomes toxic. I won't deny that stolen waters are sweet, and bread eaten in secret is pleasurable...for a while. A very short while. In the end, it always reaps a deadly toll.

Licentious sex trades short-term *pleasure* for long-term *pain*.

As I found out first hand, a person who commits infidelity is an idiot. He lacks judgment. He's destroying himself along with the people he loves. You can't walk through the fire and not get burned. It's impossible. And that is exactly what you do when you connect with a woman illicitly.

Listen to me! I know what I'm talking about. It's all vanity of vanities! A waste of time. Trust me. Pursuing the beautiful women for sex's sake will be your undoing. That, my friend, is a promise you can count on.

Don't misunderstand me. I'm not putting down beauty or sex. God created both and declared that they were good. And I also know that everybody has physical needs. Fire within a fireplace creates warmth and enjoyment for all around, but take that fire out of the fireplace and let it burn out of control and it becomes a force that can quickly destroy all that you have worked to achieve.

Also, there is a huge difference between having sex and making love. Any two animals can procreate, but it takes two souls connected deeply to *make love*. Being attracted to your partner is important, but outward beauty promises something eternal that it can never deliver, even if you are in love. Eventually everyone's looks change. Experiencing love, companionship, and commitment with your spouse is the only real option. A man who finds a wife finds a good thing and receives favor from God.

After all I've learned I'll take a wife of noble character over a stunning, outwardly beautiful woman any day. Of course it would be great to have a woman with both, but beauty and looks are passing things and fade with age.

And guess what? Your looks will fade too!

So what's the *bottom-line* on sexual pleasure? If you think getting the other woman—or *more* women—will satisfy, think again. The grass always looks greener on the other side of the fence, but the grass on that side eventually gets weeds too. Before you sneak away for a little stolen honey, consider what it might cost you in the long run.

Instead, enjoy a relationship with your wife, whom you love, while you are alive on this earth. This is God's provision. However, be warned about this also—while marriage is good and a blessing to be enjoyed, I know from personal experience that it will not *ultimately* satisfy you either. If you cling to a romantic myth, hoping to live out the "happily-ever-after" scenario, that too is vanity. There is no "happily-ever-after." Even if you are in rapturously in love with each other and deliriously happy together, eventually one will die first and you will be separated, putting an end to that.

What could be better than experiencing fine things and enjoying life to the fullest—eating, drinking, and being glad while you are still alive, happy-go-lucky and full of laughter? After all, laughter is a good medicine, is it not? What's wrong with that?

Well, I'll tell you what's wrong with it. Most of us behave like we are going to live forever. But we're not. We're all going to die, and our body will turn to dust just like every other living thing. Some of us may live longer than others. But some of us are going to die soon—sooner than we think. We don't know when we're going to die; you could die before you finish reading this book for all you know.

Yet, knowing these things, we still foolishly put death in the back of our mind and continue to spend more time planning our vacations and parties and pursuing the dreams we're convinced will fulfill our longings. We do this instead of dealing with eternal matters.

I'm going to let you in on a little secret—that long awaited vacation is not going to do it for you; neither is that new home or boat or whatever you're holding out for. Most likely, it's going to be a big let down. The depression I was experiencing was nothing new—I wasn't the first to feel that way, and I certainly won't be the last. It's common for people to experience bouts of depression after finally realizing their dreams.

That's because most of the images we create in our minds are usually *lies*—grand distortions of reality.

In addition to my sexual encounters, my pursuit of happiness through pleasure took me to all sorts of other indulgences that I was convinced would bring me some satisfaction. You name it, I did it. For instance, you may value sports cars. In my day, I had a collection of the fastest vehicles around—exotics that thundered as they raced ahead. I had not just one ship but a fleet, including a first-class luxury yacht on which I threw outrageous parties filled with magnificent entertainment and ungodly amounts of alcohol.

I never lacked for friends. In fact, they clung to my life like leeches! I was the social center of my time—*the man*. Anyone who was anyone knew *me*, and personalities rose to stardom and crashed to earth with my pleasure or displeasure.

All this did bring a certain sense of happiness. But just like sex, as I figured, eventually the enjoyment of possessions, power, and influence also faded, and my depression returned. I didn't hunger for the wind in my hair on a thundering chariot, and my yacht became more of a headache than a pleasure. The two happiest days of a man's life are the day he buys his boat and the day he sells his boat. I didn't sell mine. I simply left it in the marina to rot, abandoned and forgotten.

Possessions only complicate a person's life. Looking back, my whole affair with "stuff" was just plain silly. Someone very foolish once said, "He who has the most toys in the end wins." I say, "He who has the most toys has the biggest headaches."

And alcohol, I quickly discovered, has a similar effect as illicit sex—it only destroys. Nothing good ever comes of it. Strong drink is a mocker. You think you're doing some great deed by disbursing it generously so everybody can have a little fun, but in the end, it always comes back to bite you. Alcohol makes people do senseless things, and after they do them, they get mad, then blame you and want your money! Moderation is a virtue that very few people practice.

Hear me on this and be wise. You'd be much better off if you never get started with alcohol, and for God's sake don't give it to your friends!

And let's talk about all those "friends" (if you can call them that) with whom I partied so richly. During this time, it was difficult for me to distinguish genuine friends from those who were merely hanging around for what they could get. As long as there was plenty of alcohol, women, and entertainment to go around, friends were a dime a dozen. But the moment I became depressed again and needed someone I could actually count on, they scattered like teenagers asked to help with the chores.

Laughter is foolish, and what does pleasure accomplish? They're meaningless! I'll take one faithful friend over a thousand sycophant "friends" anytime. They're not *friends* at all. They're flatterers, "yes men" groveling about like dogs under a table begging for scraps.

If you fall down, you can count on a faithful friend to help you up. A true friend loves at all times. I'll tell you something else. *Wounds* from a true friend are preferable than all the flattery you get from the phonies. When you find a loyal friend, treat him like the gold he is, because he's truly priceless. If you don't forsake him, when disaster strikes he'll be there for you—even if your blood relatives aren't.

After all the wild partying, alcohol, drugs, boats, and fast women, my body, as well as my soul, was broken. I was weary and in poor health. Too many sleepless nights had taken their toll. (You won't see any commercials for alcohol telling how many brain cells you sacrifice for the sake of mindless oblivion!)

Realizing the negative effect my excesses were having, I then decided to change my ways, to slow down and pursue the more serene, aesthetic pleasures of life. I thought that I might find satisfaction by traveling to faraway, exotic places to take in the beauty of nature and experience the mystique of God's creation. I wanted to get away from the pressures and responsibilities of the rat race and take in long, deep breaths of fresh air, absorb the crispness, and let it cleanse my mind.

Sitting atop the highest mountain peaks in the region, the view was nothing short of awe-inspiring. The panoramic mountains stretching for hundreds of miles in every direction momentarily took my breath away. There were no sounds, save the brisk breeze whistling past and the occasional screech eagles circling in the ardent blue sky. If ever there was a place to connect with the universe and find peace of mind, this was it. The only problem was that everywhere I went, there I was—I brought all my mental and physical baggage.

If you are one of those people who live for the day when you can cut loose from the grind and spend all your time fishing or traveling, then I hate to be the one to burst your bubble. I did all that, too, and the answer is not there, either. If you are putting all your hopes in a scenic retirement, you're heading down a road that leads to disillusionment. You will be retired, old, and without purpose—and that, my friend, is a sad, sad state to be in.

Obviously, I'm not trying to say that the great outdoors and traveling weren't enjoyable or peaceful at times, but none of that came close to quenching the longing in my soul. And I'm quite certain it will not quench yours, either. This, too, I found to be ultimately meaningless.

Seeking pleasure, immoral or otherwise, is a meaningless pursuit. Immoral pleasures leave you feeling empty and guilt-ridden, while decent pleasures will just leave you empty. Remember, even too much of a good thing will eventually make you sick.

This feeling of emptiness doesn't come from being disappointed by sorrow; it comes from disappointment with *pleasure*.

LESSON 3

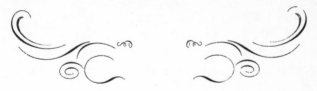

No matter how tempting—living for pleasures and possessions will never satisfy your true cravings.

CHAPTER 3

what's in a name?

Not dissuaded from my search to find the *bottom-line*, I now looked back on this indulgence in pleasure as more of a distraction than a legitimate source of satisfaction. The lures of self-gratification had pulled me in and knocked me off my main course. This happened, I supposed, because my mind had been so burned from study that the pendulum of reasoning swung in the totally opposite direction—from deep thinking to *no thinking*.

My escape into the life of hedonism had merely been a reaction to the weariness and disillusionment I had felt from my pursuit of intellectualism. Like the rest of the world, I too had longed for mind suspension—to simply put all the pain and injustice that had blasted through my façade of intellectualism out of my mind.

Yet, some of those quiet moments in nature—although they did not produce the definitive peace I had hoped for—did allow me an opportunity to reflect on how utterly mad indulging in the excesses and debauchery really had been. Though life is short to be sure, living for pleasure has no point at all. What does it accomplish other than addiction? The only lasting thing that lifestyle gave me was inflamed cravings and squandered resources. This whole pursuit of pleasure ended up no differently than my intellectual one. It too seemed like trying to catch the wind. Nothing was gained under the sun.

Having experienced about as much pleasure that I suppose a man could withstand in one lifetime, I made a concentrated effort to curtail my appetites and refocus myself. Breaking free from some of those appetites, however, proved to be a huge struggle in itself. Occupying my mind with work again helped considerably. Yet this decision to dive back into work was more than just an attempt to divert my mind. There was another compelling reason.

You see, during those years of uninhibited pleasure seeking, while I was supposedly experiencing new heights of ecstasy, my reputation was steadily on the decline. Requests for my counsel had dwindled down to a trickle. Of course, I was too wrapped up in my own self-interest to even care. Ego kept me feeding my own desires while the excesses kept me numb.

My counselors—my "yes men" or whatever you wish to call them—began informing me that a large portion of the population had become increasingly dissatisfied and distrusting with my leadership. There were even rumors floating around about a revolt. The high taxes I had levied were not particularly popular, especially in light of my lavish lifestyle. Some thought that perhaps I had gone insane and was unfit to lead. Sadly, there was a certain amount of truth in the accusations during my days of hedonism.

At any rate, those waiting in the wings for my exodus were starting to salivate while they prepared their plans for takeover. That's another thing about being in a position like mine: There is always somebody working to sabotage you or competing for your position—always somebody who thinks he can do the job better than you can. And let me tell you, when you're in the public eye, every—and I mean *every*—little thing you do gets scrutinized. And nobody looks good under a microscope.

But the threat of being overthrown didn't worry me. I remind you that I was one of the most powerful and wealthy men in all of history. I had an entire army at my disposal and could crush any attempt at revolt. The only realistic way I could lose my position would be to die, and I had paid through the nose for enough protection to keep me safe from assassination.

However, I did understand the value of a good reputation.

My whole life and career had been built on it. A good reputation carries a scent better than the most expensive cologne, while a poor reputation is like a film of scum floating on top of the perfume—its stink cancels out the sweet fragrance.

Nobody wants to have a stinking reputation; we would rather be esteemed and honored. This was one of the reasons I dove back into my work again more determined than ever before. Of course, no one should have known better than me the pure insanity of repeating the same self-defeating behaviors again and again with the same results. This time, however, all the signs indicated things would be different. I now had a new purpose for my toil. At least that is what I believed. But like a dog returning to its vomit, I was a fool destined to repeat his folly.

My new driven nature was propelled in part by a need to be liked and recognized and to do something good for the world. I would throw myself back into my work but this time to expand the nation even larger and make it stronger—to do things that would really make a difference in the world, for the betterment of humankind.

I thought perhaps this was the missing piece of the puzzle and would lead me to fulfillment and the answers that I was still determined to find.

I took on new building ventures and causes, created national parks with goliath reservoirs, and brought in events for the public. I improved the living environment for everyone by funding community projects and taking active roles in their development. I tried to identify with the "average Joe" by lowering taxes and giving incentives. I was facing the back-end of middle age and knew time was short; I wanted to make up for all the wasted years of foolish pleasure seeking and again be regarded as the greatest and wisest.

I wanted to leave a *legacy*.

This season of my life worked. Everything I touched seemed to turn to gold. The projects were successful and my popularity again soared. Awards and accolades came my way as the nation grew to even greater prominence. Other world leaders sought my counsel once again. If I lived in your era, my face would have certainly graced the covers of popular magazines such as *Time*, *Newsweek*, *Fortune*, *GQ*, and *People*. I would have done the talk show circuit (except I wouldn't have merely appeared on Oprah, I would have *owned* Oprah). Paparazzi would have pursued me twenty-four seven.

Just like Donald Trump, whose business crashed only for him to climb back to the top, I too had made a comeback. All was well...on the surface. However, despite my rise to renewed importance, the inward peace I sought was still somehow escaping me.

It was during this time that I discovered something else about people. Amazingly, they tend to forget things in your past when you are on top—particularly if you are taking care of them in the present. I learned that, for the most part, people are all about themselves. Deep down, they really don't care about your great achievements or what's going on in your life. They're actually thinking about their own needs and dreams most of the time—and if you can help them get what they want, they're happy with you. The minute you stop, you're out of their mind completely or they begin to criticize you. After a while, this began to gnaw at my insides.

Signs of my aging were becoming increasingly evident—deep grooves in my forehead, unsightly crows-feet, and graying hair. And in addition to that, I was lonely. Sometimes the top can be a very forlorn place—

even more so when you are aging. Nobody really wants to be around you unless they can get something from you. It is quite possible, I've found, to be surrounded by people and yet be entirely alone.

And I knew that I would eventually be forced to turn over all my efforts to these people who did not care for me. I had spent an entire lifetime working diligently to obtain wealth, knowledge, and expertise in order to develop great things for myself and the nation only to one day be forced to relinquish everything to people who hadn't done a solitary thing to earn it. What a rip off! It began to truly eat at me, knowing that they would inherit all my hard work.

This is not only unfair; it's stupid!

Furthermore, I began to obsess over whether or not they would continue to pursue my high standards. But really I knew they wouldn't. Everything eventually goes the way of ruin. I poured my life into my work, and I knew it would all be for nothing!

Let me ask you something to further my point: Do the names Mwene Mutapa, Hatsepshut, Jayavarman, Chandraqupta, Mansa Musa, or Qin Shihuangdi mean anything to you? Do they even ring a bell? I didn't think so. Did you know each of them was a world-renowned leader in his day? But even though they were once extremely rich, powerful, and well educated, most people haven't even heard of them! They're all long dead, their wealth squandered by others and their kingdoms in ruins. For the most part, they are long forgotten—as I imagined I would be, along with all the work that I thought was so critical.

Think about the work you are so tied up in knots about right now—that project or some precious activity you are pouring yourself into. What will be its impact a hundred years from now? Nobody's going to even remember your name—not even your great-great grandkids.

I lapsed back into despair yet again and detested my very existence, scorning my affluence and accomplishments and everything I had done to acquire a sense of purpose and peace of mind. After more than a decade of searching for the *bottom-line* truths about life, I was more depressed and confused than ever. I wondered if my search had been in vain.

But then, when all appeared lost, true enlightenment came.

LESSON 4

It's not enough to be remembered—
it's what you are remembered for that counts.

CHAPTER 4

who is really in charge?

True enlightenment, however, did eventually come to me. My long awaited breakthrough had finally arrived.

It had taken so long because it had been prevented until I came to a place that I never would have chosen to go—to the absolute end of myself. It was there; sodden with humility, disillusionment, and even more depression, that my colossal ego hit rock bottom.

I had spent all those years laboring, indulging, and probing the ways of man in hopes of finding the *bottom-line* truths of life that would fill the void in my soul. Yet instead of finding them, my journey had *led* me to the absolute end of myself.

It's important for you to know that I chose the word "led" for a specific reason. Looking back, I am fully persuaded that I did not end up at rock bottom merely by chance; rather, I was actually *led* there. Now this next statement is not going to be popular with the "positive-thinking" gurus, and I'm quite certain it will ruffle a few of those feathers I warned you about back at the beginning of this book. Nevertheless, it is the truth–possibly the first *bottom-line* truth of my entire quest.

After all my dazzling successes in life, this rock-bottom state of being at the absolute end of me is *exactly* where God wanted me to be. Instead of happiness, He desired I find brokenness; and instead of my pride, He wanted poverty of spirit. I won't lie to you. At first, this was a hard place to be in. It was a difficult pill to swallow and painfully unpleasant.

However, I am compelled to tell you that I eventually

came to see this experience as *the* greatest gift of my life–greater than any pleasure my wealth and achievements ever brought. You see, it was there, amidst the depths of my brokenness, that I was finally able to receive and comprehend the very *bottom-line* truths about life that I'd been searching so long to find.

The result of applying those truths was peace–the lasting and satisfying peace I had sought after.

Before we can go deeper in this discussion, it is vital that we are on the same page–that you understand just what I meant by hitting rock bottom and coming to the end of myself. This end of the line is not to be confused with depression or despair, although depression and despair are often there. When you come to the rock-bottom end of yourself, life ceases to be about *you*. And that is a good place to be.

Let me explain it to you another way. The main difference between where I was when I began my quest for answers and where I was when I hit my lowest point was simply this—awareness.

I had concluded all of life to be meaningless and vanity, like chasing after the wind. However, despite my depression and disappointment with life, I still looked to my own self for empowerment. I was intoxicated with my own abilities and felt that I could create change through my own strength. Now, after coming full circle I was back to the same conclusion that life was utterly meaningless. The difference was that this time I knew I was absolutely powerless to create change. I had felt a measure of strength and power, but now I was finally aware of my true powerlessness.

I was rudely awakened to the awareness that my perceptions and calculations that I had once held in such high regard were collapsing all around me. I had gone as far as I could go on my own resources. Though I hadn't run out of money, I had run out of *will*.

I was getting older, and I didn't have the energy and drive that I once had—physically or emotionally. Those that still came around for counsel soon found out that I was in worse shape than they were. I had assumed that in achieving the level of success that I had, life would be complete, but the reality was that all I wanted to do was go to sleep and never wake up.

It was at this point that I threw my hands up to God, not in prayer mind you, but because I was railing, and shouting, *"I quit! I give up my quest! I can't do it anymore. Just let me die and return to dust!"*

It seemed no sooner had I uttered those words than the Spirit of God settled in my heart and seemed to say, "It's about time. I've been waiting for you to give up. *Now* I can help you." With that, a peace I had not felt since my youth flooded my soul, and I knew I was on the right track. The answers began to come. I started a new journey—the journey from insanity back to true wisdom.

LESSON 5

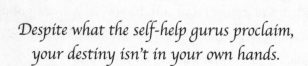

Despite what the self-help gurus proclaim,
your destiny isn't in your own hands.

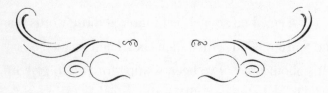

CHAPTER 5

if you're in a hole—stop digging!

"Where did I go wrong?" I had asked myself that same question years earlier, but because of my incredible success and pride I wasn't able to hear the answer. However, in my broken state, it had become crystal clear that the question was warranted after all. I had most definitely gone wrong—drastically wrong! And not only had I gone wrong, it was my own fault! Though I was "led" there by God, I knew why He had done it.

When on his deathbed, my father, also a great leader had admonished me to always follow after the "Divine Wisdom of God." If I kept God's ways before my eyes, he said, I would have *authentic* success—I would be like a tree planted firmly by the water and my leaves would never wither; I would see success in all that I set my hand to do.

Enthusiastically accepting my father's advice, I became like a sponge absorbing all of God's wisdom that I could. In the beginning, I even chose God's wisdom over money and other allurements that offered immediate gratification. It had been drilled into my brain from childhood that the fear of God was the beginning of true wisdom. Yet, as the years passed and I broke one barrier after another and achieved unparalleled pinnacles of greatness, I compromised one of the main foundations of God's wisdom—I became prideful. Pride goes before destruction and arrogance before a fall.

I allowed my ego to swell, and thought I knew better than anyone—even God. Looking to myself for solutions that I'd once asked God about resulted in even more compromise. Bit by bit, the sure and stable ways of God in my life eroded. Thus began my downward slide until eventually I was blatantly ignoring God in more outwardly defiant ways going against His specific instructions.

Moving away from God's wisdom is usually like that. It doesn't happen all at once; it happens ever so slowly, until one day you wake up and don't even recognize the person in the mirror staring back at you.

Nevertheless, despite my rebellion, I continued to have extraordinary outward success. But without even noticing, my plumb line had been detached.

When a builder is setting a foundation to a house, erecting a wall, or laying brick, he runs a long piece of string with a metal weight hanging from it called a *plumb line*. The plumb line is the most commonly used level in the world. Utilizing the earth's own gravity, it gives the builder an accurate and *true* line to which he can align his construction. If a house is built "true to plumb," it will be perfectly level and straight.

If a builder tries to construct a project relying on his own sight—though it may appear consistent to the eye—the finished work will be significantly off base and the construction uneven. And when a house is uneven, it's not only crooked—it's unstable as well.

God's wisdom is the plumb line for life. I knew this and had even counseled others that if God were not involved in the building of their house, their labor was in vain. We are to build the house of our life by utilizing the plumb line of God's wisdom, or we will have a very unstable life house in the end. It will collapse or shift, especially when strong winds beat against it during a storm.

Disregarding my own counsel had made my life unstable for years, because I had been building my house without His plumb line. I had relied on my own intellectual knowledge, and there is a colossal difference between God's *wisdom* and man's *knowledge*. It's not terribly difficult to become an intellectual, but it's awfully difficult to become *truly wise*.

Working by my own intellect and foolishness, I was like a builder lining up his construction with his naked eye—and that's pure insanity! Yet that's exactly what we do when we attempt to live our lives outside of God. Knowing what I know now, I can say with absolute confidence that the smartest men on earth without God have not even scratched the surface of real understanding. Their minds have been darkened by their own sin, and therefore their reasoning is flawed. True wisdom from above comes only through God's revelation. This is why men without God can come to such erroneous conclusions about the matters of life, just as I had done.

Living outside of God's wisdom, I had come to the mistaken conclusions that everything in life is meaningless and vanity, like trying to catch the wind. But now, with God back at the center, my understanding became illuminated and things started to come into focus. In the light of God's wisdom, I want to give you a re-analysis of my prior conclusions.

The rest of this book is about the *real* bottom lines for which I had been searching.

LESSON 6

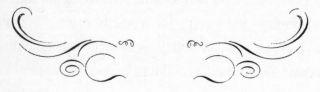

When you think you've got it all figured out and have it all together, beware: you're in trouble!

Is pursuing goals, education, achievements, or even pleasure wrong?

Of course not—unless you are pursing those things as an *end in themselves*. Nothing outside of God's plan for your life will ultimately satisfy you. If we spend our lives building our houses our own way, we will end up in an unstable state—confused, disillusioned, and unfulfilled. Life *will* be meaningless and vain.

A life like that is akin to going to all the trouble of planning and cooking a gourmet dish but leaving out all the seasonings. Yeah, it might be an edible dish. It may even look appetizing. You can place it in the finest china that money can buy, but the moment you put it in your mouth you'll find that it's tasteless and a huge disappointment. Many people's lives are like that—mine was. Beautiful things may surround them, but all that is meaningless if the main ingredient (God) is missing.

There is no lasting satisfaction or peace of mind apart from God. He is the main ingredient that makes everything work.

It's that simple.

Anything else is only an illusion. The individual who supposes he can understand life apart from God and chooses not to acknowledge Him may prosper and may find riches, but when it's all said and done, he will be terribly empty and completely disillusioned.

CHAPTER 6

your clock is ticking

Remember at the beginning when I said there are only so many seconds in a day and they are ticking away at light speed? Well, that is true—there are 86,400 seconds each day, to be exact.

We waste so much time living without God because we don't have a proper understanding of His timing and what He is doing in a particular situation. Pay extra attention to what I have to say concerning this matter, because it's a vital element for healthy living. When we view the world from God's perspective instead of merely our own intellect, we are able to discern that with Him there is a proper time, place, and season for everything and that He is ultimately in control.

There is a time to be born and a time to die; a time to sow and a time to reap. Taking life never seems to be a good thing, but at times justice requires it; other times, it is best to encourage healing and forgiveness. Sometimes tearing down is just as important as building up. Weeping has a season, as does laughter. There is a time to embrace, and there's a time to keep your distance. At times we must hold out and hold on for what we are seeking, but there are times when we must let go. There are times when we have to simplify our lives by throwing stuff out, and there is a time to store up precious things. Speaking your mind is right at times, but at others it's best to keep your mouth shut. There's a time for love and a time for hating certain things. There's a time for war and a time for peace.

Everything that happens in this world happens at the time God chooses. A sparrow doesn't fall to the ground without his knowledge. In fact, God is at work despite bad things and when we don't understand what He's doing. He doesn't *cause* things, but He works through them anyway. Nothing comes to us—good or bad—unless God first allows it; and adverse as well as positive circumstances will come upon us all.

When the uninvited and painful ones befall us, we sometimes yell out to God, "That's not fair!" But who are we to judge God? His ways are so much higher than ours. Where were we when He set the universe in motion? And though we can have a partial understanding of His ways, we will never be able to fully fathom what He has done from beginning to end.

We must trust in His faithfulness. Right now we see as through a glass, and darkly, but someday He will bring clarity, showing that everything works out according to His purposes. When you keep this in mind, you'll find contentment in knowing that God will ultimately right every wrong.

Life makes more sense when sifted through the filter of God's wisdom. If men—including me—will trust in the Lord with all their hearts and rely not on their own insight, and acknowledge Him in all their ways, He will help us make sense of the different seasons in our lives.

Now, I do recognize that much of God's "timing" is beyond our control. It's grueling to persevere when you're getting no results. On other occasions, however, you do the same thing that you've been doing all along, but this time something different happens.

It's a different season. Life unfolds on God's timetable, not ours, which often makes events harder for us to understand. And apart from His illumination, we *can't* understand. When life unravels before us, we are tempted to think that He is not in control after all. But when we view our situations through the eyes of faith and God's wisdom, light shines upon us and He eventually makes everything clear. It's important that we are careful to live our lives as wise men and make the most of the time, discerning the season, and understanding God's will.

For a moment, let's look deeper at this whole issue of *time* and *futility*. As strange as it may seem, they both go together.

Why does everything in this life fail to give any lasting satisfaction? Why do we keep bumping up against the walls of futility and disappointment when we expect the things and people to bring us so much happiness?

The answers are that everything has to do with time and futility. You see, this earth is not mankind's final home, and God created us to be *timeless* beings. God has set eternity in the hearts of men, and deep in our core we yearn for infinity—life outside of time and space as we know them. The problem is that we are fallen creatures presently constrained by time, so it's difficult for us to even comprehend eternity—even though we long for it.

And though we have come to experience death as a natural phenomenon, in reality, it is not. God did not originally create us to taste death. Death is another result of man's fallen state and the curse. God made us to live *forever*, and as a result we are not completely satisfied with this brief life.

It is by God's design that we find futility when we live apart from Him. Of course, this is not how stubborn, natural man views his endeavors at first. When he starts out, he puts all his hopes in finding happiness through his work, pleasures, relationships, and intellectual pursuits. And, as I can testify, these things do offer a degree of fulfillment in the beginning. But even though many things in life are filled with goodness and wonder—and we can experience a degree of happiness through them— they will inevitably fall short of yielding the long-term contentment for which we all hunger.

Instead of fighting against it as I did for so many years, you must learn to view this futility as a precious *gift* from God and that it is ever reminding us that we are His children, created with hearts designed to search after and to *know* Him. You may convince yourself that you are happy for a while, but deep down in your heart of hearts, you know you are not fully satisfied. You're unsatisfied because within your soul is a spark of divinity calling out for connection with your creator.

Hear me on this one, because it's the truth, and you know it. Apart from seeking to know and please God, there will be no lasting satisfaction regardless of what you do.

Life may put us in situations that our natural minds can't understand, but if we are connected with God, move in His wisdom, and have our ultimate destiny in sight, we will find that He replaces our anxiety with peace. We will see that He gives life that has a meaning beyond this world and beyond what happens to us on it. None of the things in the realm of *time* will ever fully satisfy, so stop looking to the things of time and start looking to the things of eternity. Everything else is futile.

LESSON 7

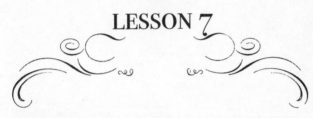

No matter how long your days on earth—
you are going to die. Better look for the eternal.

CHAPTER 7

losing God through religion

So, you think you are pretty religious because you go to temple or church or wherever? What if I told you that just as mankind pursues intellectualism, pleasure, careers, and other futile things (when they're apart from God); we do the same thing with *religion*?

We can be quite religious and still be light years away from God. I know it sounds like an oxymoron, but it's not. We can spend enormous amounts of time and energy going through hordes of rituals and not even know the God of creation. *Evil* men can be religious too. In fact, all sorts of evils have been done in the *name of religion*. History is littered with accounts of religious people doing hideous things—all in the name of God.

Religion is used as a tool for political gain, status in the community, and even to control people. Others think that God is going to view them differently because they're doing their "religious duty." They make all kinds of confessions and pious-sounding declarations, but their daily lives don't measure up to their mouths. They're more concerned about being seen by men than they are with pleasing God. Boy do they have a big surprise coming!

Look, don't fool yourself, because God sure isn't fooled. You can't impress God or be reconciled to Him by grand gestures or by making hasty and needless promises. He knows everything, including the intent of our hearts. It's best to stop talking so much and start listening more.

Knowing God is not about rituals and ceremonies—religion—as we have assumed. Rather, a life with God is about listening and living out what we've learned.

Religious rituals and sacrifices are the easy way out. You can do those things without a repentant heart. When a man's heart is deceitful, God doesn't derive any pleasure from his religious rituals.

God does desire a broken and contrite heart. That is something my father once told me that quickened in my mind after I turned away from man's pursuits and looked to God.

Religiosity only makes self-righteousness people more prideful because they hope to impress others with their outward show. They actually believe they are doing God and themselves a great favor, when in truth they are an insult to Him and defraud their own souls by their hypocritical piousness.

When you turn to God, always be alert. Consider carefully where you go and what you involve yourself with. Concentrate on having an open heart and open ears to hear what God is saying to you. Every one of us is a fallen creature with a heart capable of evil. Just as man has that spark of divinity in his nature drawing him towards God, he also has a natural bent towards evil and his own narcissism.

As I just said, God knows everything. You can't fool Him. He knows our hearts even better than we do.

LESSON 8

Being religious is no guarantee of experiencing God.

CHAPTER 8

the art of being rich—and poor

For a moment I want to revisit this whole issue of mankind's love affair with money. Although I too was once caught up in the deceptive romance myself, I now see more clearly than ever before that it is utterly insane. Money is not only a lure that snags the naive and then reels them into its hypnotic influence, but it is also a lover for whom some will quite literally sell their very soul.

Now, you're probably thinking I'm going to say that money is equal to the devil himself and it will never bring you any happiness or fulfillment–that money is evil. But that's not what I'm going to say at all, because it's not true. Money is no more evil than a computer or a television.

Computers and television have been used for great good but also great evil. It's all in how you use them.

The truth is, money can do a lot of good and create many marvelous advantages. Money fuels the economy. People need it to purchases their living essentials, such as houses, clothes, food, and gas. Money pays for educations and allows us to enjoy recreation. Money is used to build temples and churches and fund missions and other charitable causes.

And money can buy *some* happiness, bring *some* satisfaction, and give a *certain amount* of independence. It's no sin to have money, nor is it sinful to work hard for success in life and to have the things that prosperity brings.

However, reader, beware—there is another side to money. It's a darker and more sinister side, a side that forever falls short of its promises. Money can be deceitful, because it not only makes copious promises to fix people's lives; it never tells its victims that it will suck the life right out of them if they are not extremely cautious.

To be sure, those who live for the pursuit of money will never have enough. The more they get, the more it demands of them because now it costs more to live (and that only increases). As their money increases, they acquire more stuff that they think they need to make them happy. Then, the pressure is on to make even *more* money in order to sustain their lavish lifestyle. Statistics have proven time and time again that those with the highest incomes have the highest debt burden.

I'm going to tell you the truth here. I've watched both the rich and the poor, and I have concluded that *both* struggle because of money. The poor can be just as covetous as the rich. Money doesn't eliminate our problems, as the world seems to believe. But, if you are like most of the population, then you probably subconsciously buy into that idea.

The reality is that sometimes people's problems really begin when they become wealthy. The more money a person has, the more headaches he has. With riches come worries about how to *keep* them and how to avoid losing it.

Hey, I know what I'm talking about, too. I was so wealthy that my servant's servants were richer than the majority of you! And I can tell you straight up, riches don't help you sleep any better at night, as some would suggest. People think they can make themselves secure with wise investments and a horded wealth. They think they can *buy* peace of mind.

But in truth great wealth only keeps a man awake at night, tossing and turning, anxious about his money issues. I know—I've even had panic attacks in the middle of the night, and I was the richest man of my era! Money does anything *but* bring peace. It only offers a *false* sense of security.

And money has wings! It can be here today and fly away tomorrow. Absolute security can be found nowhere except in God, who alone is faithful.

Just listen to a few of the countless cries of the rich throughout history. When John D. Rockefeller was in his early fifties, he had a net worth of over a billion dollars and was earning an additional 60 million each year. You'd think he'd be one of the happiest men alive, because he was certainly one of the richest. Yet, he was constantly in poor health because of depression and insomnia due to anxiety. Do you want to know what finally helped pull him out of his depression and turn his health around? He started giving his money away!

W.H. Vanderbilt said, "The care of $200 million is too great a load for any brain or back to bear. It is enough to kill anyone. There is no pleasure in it."

Shortly before he died in 1848, John Jacob Astor, who left over 20 million to his children said, "I am the most miserable man on earth." Andrew Carnegie who said, "Millionaires seldom smile."

And who can forget the most famous rich guy of all—besides me of course—Howard Hughes? By age sixty-five, he had accumulated somewhere around 2.5 billion dollars. But listen to this—despite all that money, he lived in a room that blocked out all the sunlight. How depressing! Physically, he had let himself go to ruin, with a scraggly beard, matted waist-length hair, and fingernails over an inch long. All he did was lie in his bed naked because of his fear of germs.

Does that sound like a happy fellow? Just as I had, he came to view life as utterly meaningless. No more than a withered skeleton and addicted to chemicals, Hughes died at age sixty-seven. Interestingly, an inexpensive medical device that one of his own companies developed could have saved and prolonged his life. Tell me, what good was gaining all those riches if he lost his soul?

Another thing I've noticed is that money creates temptations that few can handle. Just take me for example. I started out with great wisdom—more than anyone around—yet in spite of it, I still came under money's intoxicating power. Here's a warning you can take to the bank: If being rich is your great goal, the temptations and lusts that drag at you will try extra hard to ambush you and ruin your life.

The love of money creates all kinds of evil scenarios and has caused many people to leave God's wisdom and fall into a life of greediness, which eventually brings them much sorrow. It takes a very special person to have riches and remain faithful to God—*very* special.

I know—you probably want to blow me off right now because you're one of the billions out there who desire to be rich, but I'm not joking about this! Like illicit sex with a beautiful woman, obnoxious amounts of money are way overrated.

Money buys artificial happiness and artificial peace. Money may get you more pleasure from life, but no amount of money will ever give you *contentment*. And that, my friend, is where the real wealth is.

If you find satisfaction in your work, consider it a great gift from God. There's really nothing better. You know, when God put Adam in the Garden of Eden before the fall, God gave him a job to do. Work is a blessing from God. It is a *good* thing.

And don't be misled about me. I thoroughly enjoyed my work. It gave me a sense of accomplishment. It just didn't bring the lasting satisfaction or peace for which I was searching. There was always something missing. It's true that you can't take your accomplishments with you when you die, but for this life, working hard does have its rewards.

Remember, it's all about perspective—what you're working for and what's driving you. Unlike the rich people who battle insomnia because of their constant money worries, the man who puts in an honest day of work will usually sleep like a baby at night.

Of course, if God blesses a man with wealth and the ability to enjoy it and stay humble, he needs to thank Him big-time, for this too is a gift. But even if you have wealth, don't put your trust in it—it's fleeting. Rather, seek God and the simple pleasures in life. Free yourself from the need to impress others or compare. Rejoice in all of God's good gifts, letting them lead you to a greater appreciation of Him. Ask God to help you use your money for good. Let Him develop an appreciation in you for the authentic riches of His Kingdom. Otherwise, you will spend your brief life consumed with chasing after possessions and positions and power and money—none of which are certain or lasting.

In a world that assesses itself according possessions that one obtains, we often fail to differentiate between the wealthy and wise.

LESSON 9

Money can buy you absolutely anything
but the things that really matter.

CHAPTER 9

i about laughed to death

Now it's time we talk about that little matter called "death." You may be tempted to skip ahead because the topic seems rather morbid or doesn't seem relevant to you—you're healthy, very much alive, and in love with life. But to the truly wise, death is not a morbid subject at all, and though he is alive, the wise man finds it vitally important to reflect on it. However, the wise man's thoughts about death should not be confused with those of someone who is fatalistic or has an infatuation with death.

Most people try to put death as far out of our consciousnesses as possible, constantly pushing it to the back of our minds. However, just like we people don't like to think about death, we don't like to think about God, either. This results in many people avoiding silence and becoming easily bored. We would much rather be distracted by entertainment, amusement, or work—anything that keeps our minds occupied.

We don't want to think about the reality of our own mortality and eventual reckoning with our Creator.

The obvious problem with this is that you *are* going to die eventually, and as I mentioned before, some of you may die sooner than you may think. Choosing not to think about it and therefore doing nothing about it—going along as if somehow you are going to cheat death and live forever—seems like utter insanity or foolishness to me.

This is why it's actually better to attend funerals than parties. Funerals bring the stark reality of our own mortality front and center in our minds. I'm convinced that God has used funerals to bring more people back to Himself than nearly any other means.

A wise person will pay careful attention to what God may be doing in his heart—and He often is doing something special at funerals. The wise person understands how fragile life is and realizes that, if not for the grace of God, it could be him—he knows that his days are few and each breath he takes is a gift from God. Part of having God's wisdom is to understand that our days are numbered.

It is remarkable how much people transform when they are suddenly aware that they are going to die soon —their whole lifestyle and way of thinking changes. Jokes aren't as funny anymore. Life's entertainments and amusements simply become hollow when held up to the light of the eternal.

A wise man lives every day as if it could be his last. This is wise, because we really *are* dying, day-by-day. Regardless of how much money or fame you have, you are going to die some day.

Here's the interesting thing. A healthy life must incorporate a proper view of death; when you are at peace with dying, you become free to really live.

Did you get that? Understanding death is a key to understanding life!

And just as God uses funerals and to get us to think about death, He can also use our pain and sorrow to draw us to Him. You see, when we go through pain and sorrow, the things of this world that we once deemed so important begin to fade and the things of real importance then come into greater focus. Pain helps us loosen our grip on this world.

Believe it or not, pain is actually a *gift*. It refines and cleanses our lives. Sorrow helps rid us of the shallow and superficial. Sometimes God allows things to happen in order to save our souls and prepare us for eternity with Him.

Look, I've seen it all. Nothing surprises me anymore. I've witnessed good, upright people getting the shaft and dying way before their prime, but I've seen the scum of the earth live on and on—way past the time even they thought they should. And because of that, here's what I have to say: Go ahead and take pleasure in the good times when you are able, but when difficulties come, don't act as though something unjust is happening to you.

Understand that God allows the good times as well as the hard times. God does this so that all people everywhere will recognize that nothing is sure in this life except Him and His truth. Knowing that truth, live life to the fullest by taking on every task that comes your way with enthusiasm, and if you fear God as you do, He will bless you.

And remember, it's not so much how you start the race of life that matters—it is how you finish. It is better to finish the race strong than to start out blazing but fizzle out before the end. Get your mind off your past—

the good *and* the bad—and focus on the finish line and on finishing with strength.

And for heaven's sake, stop mourning over the "good old days"—they really weren't all that *good*, anyway. When dealing with the pain of the present, we tend to immortalize the past, remembering things in a sentimental, glamorized way.

Learn to live in the *now* and enjoy the journey while you still can, before old age overtakes you. For some of you, being old seems far away right now. But trust me on this—the years fly by, and sooner than you think you'll look in the mirror and ask yourself, "Where did my life go?"

So go for it now! Follow your heart's desire. Give it your best shot. But keep in mind a couple things when you do: The fastest person doesn't always win the race, nor do the strong always win the fight. Having God's wisdom is wealth in itself, but it doesn't mean God will necessarily make you rich *monetarily*. Wise men are both wealthy and poor; but those with godly wisdom are rich in His blessings.

Working hard and applying the principles of success can help you attain your goals, but much of success is by chance—being at the right place at the right time. In light of that, my advice is to give it all you've got and don't let up, for you never know when opportunity will come knocking. Waiting for perfect conditions usually causes a person to get very little accomplished.

Work hard, ask God for wisdom, listen to His answers, and act on His direction and opportunities. But also be prepared for the hard times and death, because you never know when they will come knocking, either.

Give your best while you can, but keep in mind the one who created you. Include Him in your plans and walk by His wisdom. Don't let the excitement of being young allow you to forget that eventually you will have to give an account to God for everything you do. You may feel safe because you seem to be getting away with wrongdoing, but be aware that God does not always punish wrongdoing right away. A man may sin hundreds of times and think he's getting away with it, but he's not. Sin always has a residual affect. It'll eventually catch up with him.

LESSON 10

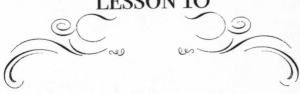

*This is the time to wake up,
smell the coffee and live!*

CHAPTER IO

i searched for God until He found me

I think by now you get the gist of what I'm trying to say. I had it all and tried it all, but nothing brought me the ultimate satisfaction I was craving until God came back into the picture. In my own stubbornness, I spent years of my life searching, determined to find the bottom-line in life. It was a long and arduous journey, though all along the wisdom of God was so near, waiting for me to just reach out and take hold of it. Simply doing so would have saved me a lot of time and suffering.

But I am no different from you and all the rest of

mankind—often, we're determined to go our own way until we hit some of the same dead ends I did. God created all men to live upright lives, yet every single one of us has turned to follow our own downward path, which will eventually end in disillusionment.

Without Him, we are destined for cynicism and empty lives. When God is enthroned in your life, however, everything becomes meaningful and significant.

So, after everything I went through and learned, what is the absolute *bottom-line* in life? It's simple but not simplistic.

✦ Be careful whom you take advice from,
because there is no end to opinions out there.

✦ Don't get caught up in the ramblings of man.

✦ Honor God in everything you do—your play,
your relationships, your money, and your work—
because this is the core reason for your creation.

✦ Enjoy life, but remember; God is going to judge
everything you do, whether good or bad—even
things done in secret.

✦ Without God, we are all foolish and doomed to
lives of regret and dissatisfaction—even me, the
wisest man to walk the earth.

- Solomon, Son of David, King of Israel

LESSON II

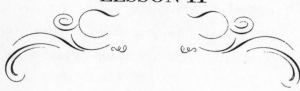

There's a time for everything, including cynicism.
But faith in God is the heart of a great life.

I applied my heart to know, to search and seek
out wisdom and the reason of things.
ECCLESIASTES 7:25

For *God* gives wisdom and knowledge and joy to a man who
is good in His sight; but to the sinner He gives the work of
gathering and collecting, that he may give to *him who is* good
before God. This also *is* vanity and grasping for the wind.
ECCLESIASTES 2:26

He who loves silver will not be satisfied with silver;
nor he who loves abundance, with increase.
This also *is* vanity.
ECCLESIASTES 5:10

Remember now your Creator in the days of your youth,
before the difficult days come.
ECCLESIASTES 12:1

For I considered all this in my heart, so that I could declare it all: that the righteous and the wise and their works are in the hand of God. People know neither love nor hatred by anything they see before them.

ECCLESIASTES 9:1

He has made everything beautiful in its time. Also He has put eternity in their hearts, except that no one can find out the work that God does from beginning to end. I know that nothing *is* better for them than to rejoice, and to do good in their lives, and also that every man should eat and drink and enjoy the good of all his labor—it *is* the gift of God.

ECCLESIASTES 3:11-13

Wisdom is better than strength, nevertheless the poor man's wisdom is despised. And his words are not heard. Words of the wise, spoken quietly, should be heard rather than the shout of a ruler of fools. Wisdom is better than weapons of war.

ECCLESIASTES 9:16-18

The patient in spirit is better than the proud in spirit.
Do not hasten in your spirit to be angry,
for anger rests in the bosom of fools.
ECCLESIASTES 6:8-9

Rejoice, O young man, in your youth, and let your heart cheer
you in the days of your youth. Walk in the ways of your heart,
and in the sight of your eyes; but know that for all these
God will bring you judgment.
ECCLESIASTES 11:9

Two *are* better than one, because they have a good reward for
their labor. For if they fall, one will lift up his companion.
But woe to him *who is* alone when he falls, for *he has* no one
to help him up. Again, if two lie down together, they will keep
warm; but how can one be warm *alone?* Though one may
be overpowered by another, two can withstand him. And a
threefold cord is not quickly broken.
ECCLESIASTES 4:9-12

It is better to hear the rebuke of the wise than for a man to hear the song of fools. For like the crackling of thorns under a pot, so is the laughter of the fool.

ECCLESIASTES 7:5-6

I know that whatever God does, it shall be forever. Nothing can be added to it, and nothing taken from it. God does it, that men should fear before Him.

ECCLESIASTES 3:14

Let us hear the conclusion of the whole matter: Fear God and keep His commandments, for this is man's all. For God will bring every good work into judgment, including every secret thing, whether good or evil.

ECCLESIASTES 12:14